I0473911

Second Edition

Employee Handbooks & "Must-Haves" for your business

THELA' R. THATCH, MBA, PHR

Edited by Avis A. Jenkins
Foreword by Elaine Martorelli

*Includes updates on the
Affordable Care Act &
Social Media in the workplace!!!*

MRS HR, LLC Publications

www.MrsHR.com

tthatch@mrshr.com

2nd edition © 2014 by Thelá R. Thatch, MBA, PHR

Design: Thelá R. Thatch

ISBN 978-1475026566

Printed in the United States of America

Employee Handbooks & "Must-Haves" for your Business

Second Edition, © 2014

CONTENTS

Foreword

Thelá R. Thatch has been a complete blessing to our school. She was our Human Resources Consultant for a year beginning in 2005 (when she was employed as a consultant for another company), until she relocated. The results of her work continue to benefit our business today in many ways. Thelá advised me through many HR processes including establishing our Employee Policy Manual, interviewing, selecting and hiring teachers and assistant teachers, state and federal law compliance, terminating employees, employee reviews, and more. As a small employer and business owner, I felt that it was necessary to educate myself and consult with a Human Resource professional. I wouldn't have thought of going it alone, as there are so many (and ever-changing) federal, state and local laws, as well as liabilities having to do with employment. At first, Thelá and I worked very closely, through phone calls, emails and weekly meetings. As new HR situations arose,

Thelá directly listened and evaluated each instance and advised me accordingly. At the same time, she provided training in different areas of HR such as establishing and implementing policies, recruiting, screening, interviewing & selecting employees, discrimination & harassment, etc.

Thelá made it a point to get to know our school operations, environment and culture. She has a beautiful, positive presence and a high level of professionalism and ethics. And at the same time, she is a down-to-earth and caring person. Not only was my work with Thelá professionally beneficial, it was an absolute pleasure to get to know and spend time with her.

Elaine Martorelli
Owner/Director
Community Montessori Academy, Verona, NJ
www.cmaverona.org

I.   What is an Employee Handbook

In a time when communication is vital to the success of any organization, businesses are consistently challenged to pay special attention to the manner by which communications are disseminated.

There are a variety of commonly used written communications employed by organizations. Some examples of these include: job descriptions, HR policy manuals, bulletins, employee handbooks, paycheck enclosures, organization newspapers /magazines, letters/memos, reports, benefits statements, training manuals, posters, newspaper ads, recruitment literature. These sources are a reflection of a business and represent how the business communicates its business goals, expectations and values to internal and external clients.

Employers can use a variety of methods to communicate policies, procedures, and work rules to employees. Employee handbooks are generally the most popular format. An employee handbook (or employee manual) is usually distributed to new employees on their first day of work. It explains major human resource and employee policies, as well as procedures which generally describe the aggregate benefits program provided to the employee.

Employee handbooks detail guidelines, expectations and procedures of a business or company to its employees. Typically, employee handbooks are given to employees at the beginning of their employment with the organization to introduce them to the organization's culture and policies. A well written employee handbook sets the foundation for a healthy business. If your employee handbook is created properly, it can effectively communicate your company's policies and procedures in a coherent and centralized manner.

However, if done inadequately, your employee handbook may become a human resource disaster. There are no set regulations or guidelines for the format of employee handbooks; therefore, you are free to design your handbook to fit your company's needs. The most effective employee handbooks share three essential qualities; content, clarity, and consistency.

There are numerous disasters and potential legal ramifications companies may encounter when they decide not to pursue an employee handbook. Sexual harassment, discrimination and other charges are prevalent, and without a clearly written "zero-tolerance policy," your company may be open to devastating fines, charges, and lawsuits. Even if you have an employee manual, if it has not been updated in over a year, it can be equally detrimental-- and possibly worse than having no manual at all.

Employee Handbooks vs. Policy Manuals

An employee handbook is written with employees as the intended audience. It is most often written using a straightforward layout for easy referencing of company policies and procedures and is a vehicle for familiarizing employees with basic company policies and benefit programs, as well as the general expectations of the company, including acceptable and unacceptable behavior and disciplinary measures.

A policies and/ or procedures manual is a comprehensive text that details every aspect of company policy, the procedures for following those policies and the forms needed to complete each process. A policies and procedures manual is a reference tool for managers and supervisors. This tool is much more complete in detail than the employee handbook and should be used for back-up when more information is needed to explain a policy or when a deeper understanding of a process is desired. As a benefit to management, the manual can contain references to federal and state laws that correlate to each policy. Managers and supervisors then have access to the rationale for the policies, thus providing them with assistance for enforcement An employee handbook is written with employees as the intended audience. An employee handbook is a vehicle for familiarizing employees with basic company policies and benefit programs, as well as the general expectations of the company. Employees learn what behaviors are acceptable and unacceptable and the disciplinary measures that result from those behaviors.

A policy and/or procedure manual is a comprehensive text that details every aspect of company policy, the procedures for following those policies and the forms needed to complete each process. A policies and procedures manual is a reference tool for managers and direct supervisors. This tool is much more detailed than the employee handbook and should be used for back-up when more information is needed to explain a policy or when a deeper understanding of a process is desired.

Why Create an Employee Handbook

Federal and state laws and the growing number of cases of employee related litigation against management strongly suggest that a written statement of company policy is a business necessity for companies of any size. For example, the United States Equal Employment Opportunity Commission reported that in 2005, companies paid out more than $378 million dollars in discrimination non-litigated settlements. In 2013, the EEOC received a total of 93,727 discrimination charges filed against private businesses.

There is tremendous value in having an employee handbook. Your handbook can serve as protection against lawsuits, discrimination cases and job actions against your company.

For example, a company in Seattle was struggling with an employee that was not meeting performance expectations. The firm accessed her e-mail on the server, and found that she was instant messaging family members. According to a company source, it turned out she was spending fifty percent of her time on e-mail. Fortunately, their employee handbook clearly stated that e-mail is an asset of the company and personal use had to be limited. The company ended up terminating the employee.

In December 2009, a former Abercrombie & Fitch and Hollister Co. manager-in-training said the store violated her religious rights by not exempting her from the store's dress code. A Federal Jury maintained that the employer had the right to enforce its own rules and regulations - including the so-called "Look Policy" that calls for its sales associates to dress in Hollister or Hollister-like clothing. That meant low-cut tops, short skirts, ripped jeans and other form-fitting clothing. The St. Louis-based jury entered a defense verdict in the lawsuit the Equal Employment Opportunity Commission filed against J.M. Hollister LLC and were pleased that a jury of eight found that Abercrombie & Fitch and Hollister Co. did not discriminate against the employee nor did they fail to accommodate her religious beliefs. The verdict was strongly based on the fact that the employee agreed to the dress code located in the employee handbook when she was hired, before converting to a faith that disagreed with the company's policies.

What to Include

An employee handbook may include (but is not limited to) the categories and items shown in Figure 1.

Category	Sample Items
Introductory Information	<ul><li>Letter of welcome from the CEO or President</li><li>Mission, vision and values</li><li>Company History</li><li>Equal Employment Opportunity Statement</li><li>Americans with Disability Act policy statement</li><li>Anti-harassment policy</li><li>Sexual harassment policy</li></ul>

Employment Information	• Terms of the initial employment period • Employment classification • Scheduled work week • Code of Conduct • Immigration Reform and Control Act (IRCA) • Transfers and promotions • Outside employment policy • Social Media Policy
Compensation	• Performance management provisions • Payment of salary • Overtime pay • Time records • Employee referral program
Time Off	• Holidays, Vacation, Sick Days • Jury duty • Bereavement • Time off to vote (Local &

	National voting policy) • Absence due to illness • Leave of absence without pay • Leave under the Family and Medical Leave Act (FMLA) • Military leave • Child-care leave policy • Parental leave policy
Employee Benefits	• Health insurance • Dental insurance • Flexible Spending Account (FSA) • Group life insurance • Short term disability insurance • Retirement/pension plan • 401(k) plan or 403(b) program • Workers' Compensation benefits

Other Information	• Attendance, punctuality, and dependability expectations
	• Drug and alcohol abuse
	• Employee Assistance Program (EAP)
	• Appearance and conduct
	• Violence in the workplace policy
	• Accidents and emergencies procedures
	• Open-door policy

(Fig. 1)

Deciding what to include in your employee handbook can be a challenge. It is important that you include enough information so that it will be useful to employees. However, your employee handbook should not include so much verbiage that it limits and places constraints on your company's actions.

Employee handbooks typically include information about company policies such as work hours, dress codes, safety & emergency procedures, vacation time, sick days, paid holidays and other fringe benefits. Some companies also choose to include information about computer usage, phone usage, and non-harassment policies.

Include a Code of Conduct section where you describe in plain language how you expect your employees to behave. Your handbook should contain crystal clear policy descriptions written in one voice. Some companies solicit various departments to contribute to the handbook lending to inconsistency and confusion.

Establish policies on maternity and family leave, bereavement, sick days and leave. There are strict federal rules on issues like jury and military duty. Make certain your employees know you comply.

Be aware that the material in your employee handbook is fair game in the courts. Including disclaimers in your employee handbook may assist in mitigating your legal risk. One of the most common disclaimers is a general disclaimer clearly stating that the handbook is not an employment contract.

An employee handbook may cover a wide variety of items and include information specific to an organization, however, there are some fairly universal considerations about compiling a successful one.

- **Keep it simple**. Handbooks should be clearly written and organized so all employees can understand them

- **Keep it current.** Handbooks must be kept up-to-date. Consider putting your employee handbook online for increased ease of maintenance and distribution.

- **Distinguish between company-wide policies and job specifics.** An employee handbook should make the distinction between information that applies to everyone in the company and procedures that relate specifically to how an employee performs an individual job.

- **Accommodate special language requirements.** Make accommodations for translating the handbook for employees who speak English as a second language. Be sure to use a professional translator since the handbook could be considered a legal document.

- **Control how the handbook is distributed.** Each employee that receives an employee handbook should sign a statement acknowledging the receipt of the document and an understanding of its contents.

- **Create a professional and appealing look.** Make sure your handbook is written by someone with a strong writing background and that it clearly communicates the information. Add graphics to add appeal and to engage employees to read the contents of the book.

Again, it is not required for an employer to have a written employee handbook; however, many employers find them to be a valuable management tool. Handbooks promote uniformity in how you treat your employees. Larger employers with several layers of management can benefit from having an employee handbook because it will act as a reference for frequently asked questions. These frequently asked questions can all be answered in a consistent and uniformed way when referred to the employee handbook. This in turn improves morale and frees the employer from a stream of requests for special treatment.

Handbooks are a convenient source of information for job applicants and new hires, as well as existing employees. They promote efficiency and they help to establish an institutional culture. They set out rules of workplace behavior which, if willfully violated and result in termination, can prove to be a defense to an unemployment insurance claim or an abusive discharge suit. Finally, they provide evidence of employer compliance with law in areas such as workers' compensation, equal employment and sexual harassment. Employers who choose to have an employee handbook should not overlook the requirements below.

- If the handbook describes leave policies and the employer is covered by the FMLA, the handbook must include a description of extended leave benefits under FMLA.

- An employer must have a written sexual harassment policy to be able to defend against sexual harassment charges.

When distributing employee handbooks to employees, have each employee sign an acknowledgement that he or she has received the handbook and will read it. Such acknowledgements are helpful in meeting an employee's claim that he or she was unaware of a particular policy or procedure contained in the handbook.

The disadvantages are that an employee handbook or similar statement of policy might be considered a unilateral contract. That is, a one sided offer by the employer to abide by the provisions of the handbook that the employee accepts simply by working for the employer. In other words, courts may treat a poorly worded handbook as an 'at-will employment contractual relationship' that limits an employer's right to fire. An employer who wishes to adopt an employee handbook but who does not want to be contractually bound by its provisions can take steps to reduce, if not eliminate, the risk of contractual liability.

Employee Handbook Considerations – To reduce the risk of being contractually bound by your employee handbook, consider the following:

- Include prominent disclaimers that the handbook is not a contract of employment and is not intended to change the at-will status of any employee
- State that the handbook is intended only as a convenient source of information about the company and its current practices and procedures, which are subject to change at any time without prior notice;
- State that employees are free to resign at any time and that the company is free to discharge an employee at any time, with or without cause;
- State that the company is not bound to

follow any particular disciplinary procedures and that the company need not be consistent in imposing discipline;

- Avoid statements such as the company "promises" or "guarantees" or will take specified action in certain circumstances; and

- Avoid any requirement that employees sign an agreement to comply with or be bound by the handbook.

In addition to an employee handbook, some companies have a managers-only manual, distributed only to managers, setting out required procedures for them to follow for discrimination complaints, discipline, termination, and so on, involving their subordinates. By placing procedural requirements in a managers-only manual, rather than the employee handbook, makes it more difficult for rank-and-file employee to claim that the company is contractually obligated to follow the procedures.

One Size Does Not Fit All

In order to guard your organization against employee lawsuits it is imperative that your employee handbook is reviewed by an attorney and customized for each state your organization does business. State laws may be different. For example, a Florida Handbook should not be used in California.

Since handbooks contain policy statements, they often become evidence in employment matters, including charges and court cases. Although they are a key in preventing and responding to discrimination, harassment, retaliation, and other claims, they also can be a double-edged sword for the employer. Whereas they can serve in any given case as the organization's best friend, they can also become its worst nightmare, depending on the way that they are written, interpreted and applied.

Make your handbook specific to your organization by reflecting upon frequently asked questions you encounter from employees during the planning period. This will ensure that the handbook is an effective communications tool and reinforces the organizational culture. Think through "What if..." scenarios while developing your policies. Ask yourself if the content in your handbook will be understood by your employee population. Decide if the handbook should be written in a more formal or informal style. Be aware of wording that creates an authoritarian tone and recognize the implication the tone may have on your business' culture.

Think carefully about who you select to write your handbook. It is preferable to have a person with human resources experience directly involved. Use an internal human resource professional, external consultant or an employment attorney. Regardless of who you use, it is highly recommended that an attorney review the handbook upon completion.

Make sure you implement policies that confirm the organization's intent to comply with applicable employment laws. Your employees know their rights; make sure you confirm that you do too!

In addition, examine your organization's status as a public or private-sector employer, since laws may not be applicable to both. Recognize that the handbook will need to be revised as changes occur. Decide who will be responsible for monitoring policies to ensure that changes and revisions are identified.

How to Distribute

Communication is **CRUCIAL**.

Distribution of your employee handbook should be a major event within your company. Create an Employee Handbook Rollout week in which your human resource partners or managers can spend time distributing the handbook to employees.

Review each section of the handbook and allow employees to ask questions.

Laws and regulations change year to year,

so it is important to review your handbook yearly to make sure that it is current. For example, in 2014, Obama directed the Department of Labor (DOL) to propose revisions to modernize and streamline the existing overtime regulations. In this order, the President insisted that the DOL consider how the current regulations could be revised to update existing protections consistent with the intent of the Act; address the changing nature of the workplace; and simplify the regulations to make them easier for both workers and businesses to understand and apply." Although this change may not take place immediately, employers must now consider taking some proactive steps, such as retaining outside counsel to perform a wage-and-hour audit, to spot issues now, limit exposure, and reduce the risk of future litigation.

Section I

"Must Haves" to Remember...

- An Employee Handbook details guidelines, expectations and procedures of your business to your employees. It can protect your company!

- ***Employee Handbooks*** are written for all employees as the intended audience. ***Policy Manuals*** are reference tools to provide standards for managers and direct supervisors.

- An Employee Handbook can protect your company against lawsuits, discrimination cases and job actions.

- Include information and policies relevant to your employees. Avoid excessive verbiage that places constraints on your company actions.

- Employee Handbooks should be written by a human resources professional and reviewed by an attorney.

- Confirmation that employees have received the Employee Handbook is critical.

- Review your Employee Handbook annually .

II.   The Evolution of Human Resources

The Beginnings of Human Resources

Businesses have existed for thousands of years. However, the practice of management itself has only been of special interest for about 100 years. The Industrial Revolution of the eighteenth century sparked a greater interest in business growth and expansion. During this time, large-scale business operations began to emerge throughout Europe and the United States. For example, as businesses became more complex and as their hiring needs became more complicated, the tasks of hiring new employees became too time consuming for a first-line supervisor or an office manager to perform. In the past, companies did not use any human resource value added processes. Human Resources consisted of hiring employees and dealing with issues and requests.

The second rapid development of Human Resources started in the beginning of 20th century. The personnel department had large responsibilities such as dealing with issues and introducing new law requirements. It had the responsibility for the implementation of different social and work place safety programs. Everything was focused on the productivity of employees. Significant change was introduced after the Second World War due to military developing training programs for new soldiers. After the war, the training became a respected process in personnel department.

The HR Revolution began in the 1970's when technology and globalization began to change the rules of the game. Now, most HR Functions are running complex HRIS solutions, which make information about employees available anywhere and anytime to managers and HR Professionals.

Human Resources in the 21st Century

The 21st century has provided a fantastic opportunity for Human Resources and businesses. Managers and leaders have to think global today;

they have to relate to different cultural backgrounds.

As social and market dynamics change, dramatic advances in technology also affect how we manage human resources. In recent years, the popularity of the Internet has profoundly affected the Human Resource Management function, and those effects are still developing and growing.

The Affordable Care Act & Your Business

The Patient Protection and Affordable Care Act (PPACA), commonly called the Affordable Care Act (ACA) or "Obamacare," is a United States federal statute signed into law by President Barack Obama on March 23, 2010. Together with the Health Care and Education Reconciliation Act, it represents the most significant regulatory overhaul of the U.S. healthcare system since the passage of Medicare and Medicaid in 1965.

The ACA was enacted with the goals of increasing the quality and affordability of health insurance, lowering the uninsured rate by expanding public and private insurance coverage, and reducing the costs of healthcare for individuals and the government. The law also requires insurance companies to cover all applicants within new minimum standards and offer the same rates regardless of pre-existing conditions or sex.

Under the ACA, employer-provided coverage is considered "affordable" if it meets one of the three IRS safe harbors for determining if the employee's contribution for self-only coverage doesn't exceed 9.5 percent of the employee's household income:

o Employee's required premium co-share for the lowest-cost, self-only coverage that provides minimum value is not greater than 9.5 percent of an employee's W-2 taxable (Box 1) income. This calculation excludes any employer contribution made to an employee's health savings account, as well as employer contributions to 401(k) plans or other nontaxable Section 125 (cafeteria plan) benefits.

o Employee's required premium co-share for the lowest-cost, self-only coverage that provides minimum value is not greater than 9.5 percent of rate of pay as of the first day of the coverage period.

o Employee's required premium co-share for the lowest-cost, self-only coverage that provides minimum value is not greater than 9.5 percent of the federal poverty level for a single individual.

Coverage is considered to provide "minimum value" if:

o The plan covers at least, on average, 60 percent of an employee's medical expenses.

The ACA's employer mandate to provide health care is known formally as the "shared responsibility" provisions, and informally as "play or pay."

If an employer does not provide a plan that is "affordable" with at least "minimum value" coverage, the employee can shop for insurance through a public exchange and may qualify for federal tax credits. Employers that are midsize (the equivalent of 50 to 99 full-time workers based on a 30-hour work week) and large (100+) will face penalties starting at $2,000 per employee, after adjustments, if they fail to provide "affordable" coverage and have employees that receive federal tax credits to purchase exchange-based coverage.

Some deadlines:

- **Starting Jan. 1, 2014**, nongrandfathered, fully insured plans in the individual and small group markets and those in the exchanges were required to provide coverage of benefits or services in 10 separate categories that reflect the scope of benefits covered by a typical employer plan. Self-insured small group plans, large group plans, and grandfathered plans are not required to offer essential health benefits.

To clarify, **small employers (that's 50 or fewer full-time employees) are not required to provide health care to their workers**, but if they do, the plans they offer must provide the above essential health benefits (and meet other specifications), unless, as also mentioned, the plans are self-insured or grandfathered.

- **Starting Jan. 1, 2015,** employers with the equivalent of 100 or more full-time employees must offer "affordable" care that meets minimum value specifications (as determined by minimum value calculations) to 70 percent of their full-time employees, to fulfill the employer mandate. By 2016, large employers will need to provide coverage to at least 95 percent of their full-time workers.

- **Starting Jan. 1, 2016,** employers with the equivalent of 50 to 99 full-time employees may face penalties if they do not provide "affordable" care to at least 95 percent of their full-time employees as specified.

These deadlines are as of February 2014, when the Treasury Department issued its most recent mandate delay via a new final rule and related fact sheet and Q&A on Employer Shared Responsibility Under the Affordable Care Act. Due to constant revisions to the ACA, please visit http://www.whitehouse.gov/healthreform

for updates as they occur.

Social Media & Your Handbook

Social media and the National Labor Relations Board have created many changes in the way your company will do business. Facebook, LinkedIn, Twitter and other social media sites have become a free for all for employees to voice their positive and negative opinions about their employers.

The National Labor Relations Board is an independent federal agency vested with the power to safeguard employees' rights to organize and to determine whether to have unions as their bargaining representative. The agency also acts to prevent and remedy unfair labor practices committed by private sector employers and unions.

In an advice memo dated May 30, 2012, a case was submitted for advice on whether the Employer's social media policy was unlawfully overbroad, and whether the Employer violated Section 8(a)(1) of the National Labors Relations Act (NLRA) by terminating the employee for posts submitted on Facebook.

Section 8(a) (1) states that it shall be an unfair labor practice for an employer "to interfere with, restrain, or coerce employees in the exercise of the rights guaranteed by section 7. It is important to know that the NLRA, Section 7 provides "employees shall have the right to self organization, to form, join, or assist labor organizations, to bargain collectively through representatives of their own choosing, and to engage in (or refrain from) concerted activities for the purpose of collective bargaining or other mutual aid or protection."

Basically, a company rule is unlawful if it explicitly restricts Section 7 activities. If the rule does not explicitly restrict protected activities, it will violate the Act only upon a showing that: (1) employees would reasonably construe the language to prohibit Section 7 activity; (2) the rule was promulgated in response to union activity; or (3) the rule has been applied to restrict the exercise of Section 7 rights.

The Board found that a rule proscribing "negative conversations" about managers that was contained in a list of policies regarding working conditions, with no further clarification or examples, was unlawful because of its potential chilling effect on protected activity. On the other hand, the Board found that a rule forbidding "statements which are slanderous or detrimental to the company" which appeared on a list of prohibited conduct including "sexual or racial harassment" and "sabotage" would not be reasonably understood to restrict Section 7 activity. In that context, "employees would not reasonably believe that the rule applies to statements protected by the Act because it was listed alongside examples of egregious misconduct.

Considering the above principles, the Board concluded that the employer's social media policy was not ambiguous because it provided sufficient examples of prohibited conduct so that, in context; employees would not reasonably construe the rules to prohibit Section 7 activity.

For instance, the employer's rule against "inappropriate postings that may include discriminatory remarks, harassment and threats of violence or similar inappropriate or unlawful conduct" is not unlawful.

Statements such as "Be Respectful" are not unlawful. However, In certain contexts, the rule's exhortation to be respectful and "fair and courteous" in the posting of comments, complaints, photographs or videos, could be overly broad. The bottom line is that the company rule should provide sufficient examples of plainly egregious conduct so that employees would not reasonably construe the rule to prohibit Section 7 conduct. The employer has a legitimate basis to prohibit such workplace communications, but must do so without burdening protected communications about terms and conditions of employment.

In addition, the employer's rule requiring employees to "maintain the confidentiality of the employer's trade secrets and private and confidential information" is also not unlawful. employees have no protected right to disclose trade secrets. Moreover, the employer's rule provides sufficient examples of prohibited disclosures. Read more about this ruling at http://www.nlrb.gov.

Avoiding Lawsuits

Businesses are named as defendants in employee lawsuits for a wide variety of reasons, but usually these lawsuits arise as a result of employees or employment candidates feeling that they have been treated unfairly by their employers.

Common examples of filed lawsuits include:

- Employees alleging that they were not hired ("wrongful refusal to employ") or not promoted ("wrongful failure to promote"), even though they were the most qualified candidate for the position, resulting from discrimination by the employer on the basis of race, color, religion, sex, national origin, age, or sexual orientation. Employees alleging that they were sexually or otherwise harassed by another employee and that management did not take action to prevent or stop the harassment.

- Mentally or physically disabled employees alleging that an employer failed to take reasonable steps to accommodate their special needs.

- Employees alleging that they were wrongfully disciplined or discharged ("wrongful termination") as a result of discrimination on the part of the employer.

- Employees alleging breach of employment

contract when terminated by the employer for any reason.

The financial consequences of employment-related lawsuits can be very severe. A painful lesson learned by many employers is that insurance coverage's typically purchased, such as General Liability and Workers' Compensation insurance; generally do not provide any coverage for lawsuits resulting from employment-related issues.

When analyzed quantitatively, the statistics related to employment-related lawsuits are staggering:

- There are currently 25 Federal laws and hundreds of state regulations addressing workplace relationships and practices;

- According to *USA Today*, 450 such lawsuits are filed in the United States each day;

- The average cost of defense for the employer in those cases in which the employer wins the judgment exceeds $30,000. In many cases the defense costs are $100,000 or more.

- Fifty-six percent of all cases tried result in verdicts for the employee-plaintiff, with the average verdict exceeding $250,000. In addition, 15% of all verdicts top $1,000,000.

- After Texas and California, the largest numbers of employee lawsuits are filed in Florida.

- The most common targets for federal discrimination claims are private companies employing between 15 and 100 employees.

Employee handbooks, when written properly, will reinforce in writing that the organization is committed to the adhering to Federal and State laws and to protecting the rights of the employee. A documented commitment to "do the right thing" can save a company millions in court and court fees.

Section II

"Must Haves" to Remember...

• The need for human resources management became apparent as organizations began to grow and become more complex.

• Social and market dynamics along with technology affect how human resources is managed.

• The Affordable Care Act was enacted with the goals of increasing the quality and affordability of health insurance. Your business will be held accountable and must know how this applies to your employees.

• Social Media has changed the landscape. However, not all employee postings are protected by law.

• Avoiding lawsuits is a daily event. Take preventive action by having an Employee Handbook and a competent human resource professional within your organization.

III.   You're hired

Once an employee is hired there are numerous best practices to have in place. In an attempt to keep it simple, I have included the "must-haves" that I have experienced to be the most needed, most used providing the company with the most leverage. Policies such a performance appraisals, benefits, progressive discipline, and safety policies are "must-haves" to make sure your operation runs smoothly.

Performance Appraisals

Performance appraisals allow an opportunity for two-way communication between an employee and that employee's direct report. The performance review process serves as a tool to share goals and expectations. Performance appraisals will assist managers when differentiating between high, mediocre and low performers. They also provide a baseline to distribute rewards, recognition and discipline accordingly. On the other hand, performance appraisals allow a company to show through documentation that someone was discharged for poor performance. For example, if an employee claims they were unlawfully fired because of their age or their race, an effective performance appraisal can show that the person was legally fired for poor performance. Without effective performance appraisals, it can be difficult for a company, a manager or a supervisor to explain to a court or government agency that a person was fired for performance related issues. It may also be difficult for a supervisor to explain to in-house company managers why a poor performer must be discharged if there is no written evidence of past performance problems.

For example, one of the worst positions a company can find themselves in is to fire an employee for poor performance, but have ten years of appraisals that rate the employee as a worker that has met expectations.

Performance appraisal records are one of the first things employee lawyers or government agents will look at when investigating a termination. Performance appraisals that do not accurately show a record of declining performance or poor performance can be used against a company in several ways. Appraisals that are inconsistent with a company's explanation of a firing will often allow a case to go before a jury. Appraisals that show a record of good performance can give the fired employee enough evidence to get into court. In addition, juries get to look at the performance appraisals.

Common errors with performance appraisals are supervisors who want to be a friend to employees. Due to this, the supervisor does not honestly tell someone that he or she is doing a bad job.

Another common error is not spending enough time on the performance appraisal to carefully describe the level of an employee's performance. A supervisor may write inflated descriptions of performance that make people appear to be far better performers on paper than they are in reality. On the other hand, the supervisor may accurately describe an employee's performance in many separate categories on the appraisal form, but then give an overall performance rating that exceeds what is written in the individual sections.

Lastly, it is important to describe the employee's performance in objective language and in terms that are related to the job. For example, instead of a manager saying that a female employee should "take a class in charm school" it would have been better to say that the employee "lacked interpersonal skills."

Benefits

Some of the most common benefits companies offer are paid vacations, employee health insurance plans, paid sick leave, disability insurance, tuition reimbursement, pension plans, life insurance, dental insurance.

Human Resource professionals have the daunting task of providing an assortment of human resources benefits that may include paid vacations, medical benefits, dental benefits, and health & wellness plans.

A good benefits plan can include many additional perks that offer true tangible gains in relation to the competition. An employee benefits package includes all the benefits provided by an employer. Employers are required by federal and state laws to provide some types of employee benefits like unemployment, workers compensation and disability.

Other human resources benefits may be provided by employers because they feel socially responsible to their employees and opt to offer them more than is required by law. Depending on the company, these benefits may include health insurance, dental insurance, vision care, life insurance, paid vacation leave, personal leave, sick leave, child care, fitness, a retirement plan, and other optional benefits offered to employees and their families.

Human resources benefits are an important part of a compensation package. A good benefits package can add as much as 30 percent to an employee's overall compensation.

Employee benefits might include relocation assistance, medical, prescription, vision and dental plans, health and dependent care flexible spending accounts, retirement benefit plans (pension, 401(k), 403(b), group-term life and long term care insurance plans, legal assistance plans, and possibly other miscellaneous employee discounts.

Some human resources benefits such as flexible spending accounts, 401(k)'s, and 403(b)'s may be excluded from the employee's gross income and are not subject to federal income tax in the United States. Some function as tax shelters. Fringe benefits are also thought of as the costs of keeping employees other than salary. These benefit rates are typically calculated using fixed percentages that vary depending on the employee's classification and often change from year to year.

Corporations may also offer cafeteria plans as human resources benefits to their employees who offer a menu and level of benefits for employees to choose from. In most instances, these plans are funded by both the employees and by the employer.

The portion paid by the employees for their benefits are deducted from their gross pay before federal and state taxes are applied. Some benefits would still be subject to the FICA tax, such as 401(k) [2] and 403(b) contributions; however, health premiums, some life premiums, and contributions to flexible spending accounts are exempt from FICA.

Employee human resources benefits provided through ERISA are not subject to state-level insurance regulation like most insurance contracts, but employee benefit products provided through insurance contracts are regulated at the state level. However, ERISA does not generally apply to plans by governmental entities, churches for their employees, and some other situations.

For more guidance on benefits administration, visit www.mrshr\benefitsproviders to locate a licensed benefits provider that will meet the needs of your organization.

Progressive Discipline

The nature and purpose of progressive discipline is based on the idea that employees deserve the opportunity to understand what is expected of them in terms of performance and behavior.

A warning notice is a tool used to explain to employees what is unacceptable and to give them the opportunity to change their behavior or performance through corrective action. Progressive discipline may vary due to the environment.

Progressive discipline systems are designed to spot potential employment problems, such as excessive absences, excessive tardiness and misconduct early on and to give the employee every opportunity to improve or change the behavior before facing dismissal. It is important to remember that the object is to get positive behavior change results, rather than to punish the employee.

Giving an employee the chance to work out the problem very often produces better results than punishment or penalties. Systems designed to punish are much more likely to be viewed by employees as arbitrary and unfair than those designed to educate and correct. That is in part because disciplinary systems designed to educate and correct are less likely to use discharge as a form of discipline the employee has been disciplined less severely in a series of progressive steps. A progressive system also shows that the employer is not trying to get rid of the employee at the first sign of a problem, which may encourage the employee to work with the employer to eliminate the problem.

Follow these steps in exercising progressive discipline with an employee:

Prior to the Meeting

- Arrange to meet with the employee privately. **Do not discipline an employee in public or in front of other workers.**

- Prepare for the meeting by reviewing your notes and files about both the specific incident or problem in question and any past discipline taken, either verbal or written.

During the Meeting

- Explain to the employee why you've called the meeting if the employee doesn't know already.

- State the specific problem in terms of actual performance and desired performance.

- Review your progressive discipline policy/program with the employee, and explain what steps have been taken already and what the next step is.

- Give the employee a chance to respond, explain and defend his or her actions.

- Acknowledge the employee's story and be sure to include it in your notes of the discipline session.

- Tell the employee that you expect his or her behavior to change. Give specific examples and suggestions.

- Indicate your confidence in the employee's ability and willingness to change the behavior.

- Have the employee repeat back to you or otherwise confirm that he or she understands the problem and is clear on what changes are expected.

- Explain to the employee that you will write a memo summarizing the session as documentation.

- Reassure the employee that you value his or her work and that you want to work with the employee to make sure that he or she can continue to work at your business.

After the Meeting

- Using your notes from the session, write a memo or other documentation that summarizes the conversation.

- If a written warning has been issued, be sure to give the employee the opportunity to sign any documentation for the file.

- Give the employee a copy of the document no later than the end of the day following the conversation.

- If the employee has other supervisors, distribute copies to them, but emphasize that the information is confidential and not to be shared with anyone else.

- Monitor the employee's behavior and performance to make sure that the problem has been corrected.

After a discipline session, you will want to make some documentation based on your notes. Use this checklist to make sure you include everything you need in your documentation.

Safety

Human Resource Management experts are being asked more frequently to manage the safety function. While this change isn't new for some organizations, it is a significant structural and functional shift for others.

Safety performance is about people. People must be motivated so that they are focused, alert and working to continuously improve. It requires leadership, commitment, and engagement.

A focus on safety and emergency planning is critical for the workplace.

Visit http://www.osha.gov/SLTC for safety and health Topics pages providing access to selected occupational safety and health information. The OSHA website also includes specific workplace hazards, as well as individual industries. Numerous OSHA and non-OSHA references are evaluated on a given subject to determine which are considered most important in reducing occupational injuries and illnesses. OSHA's Safety and Health Topics Pages provide assistance for complying with OSHA standards, enabling employers to ensure safer workplaces.

Section III
"Must Haves" to Remember...

• Performance Appraisals are opportunities for two-way communication between an employee and their direct reports. Helps to avoid "surprises."

• Benefits can create a competitive edge for your organization and build morale.

• Progressive discipline is an effective tool to coach and counsel employees.

• A focus on safety and emergency planning is critical for the success of your business.

IV.   You're Fired

Unfortunately, there will be times when your employee will need to part ways with you. I have highlighted some fundamental "need to knows" when going through this uncomfortable time of releasing an employee from employment.

No Surprises

Employees should have received enough communication regarding their performance so that there termination is not a surprise. In my experience, employees often know when they have pushed the limit and when they are near termination.

For example, while serving as a human resources consultant for a manufacturing plant that had an extremely high turnover I experienced many situations where employees hand over their company property before they were officially terminated to avoid the embarrassment of being terminated because they knew they should have been terminated due to the blatant violation of company policies.

Document, document, document!

Realtors often stress the importance of location, location, location. Human resources professionals and business owners scream the importance of documentation, documentation, documentation!

Lack of documentation can create the most stress during a termination. The fear that comes from not knowing if you are doing the right thing or if the employee will retaliate almost always stems from not having the supporting documentation that shows that the employee is being terminated due to a violation of a written policy.

Exit Interviews

Exit interviews are a great opportunity to provide a two-way communication if the employee will participate in the interview. Exit interviews can be a valuable source of information beyond learning the reasons why employees are leaving your company. When exit interviews are done well, they can uncover issues that can be addressed before they turn into lawsuits - issues such as harassment, discrimination and workplace violence. They can also provide information on how to improve procedures and can identify the programs in the company that are highly valued. Exit interviews can provide you with honest, focused feedback that you can act upon in your own time frame.

The best time to conduct exit interviews is a day or two before the employee's last day. Employees are more likely to be forthcoming with their feedback when they've worked through most of their notice period and are less fearful that their feedback will be reported back to their manager while they are still employed.

Please note that exit interviews are only appropriate for employees who made the decision to leave and voluntarily resigned. Or, for employees who elected to retire, perhaps earlier than expected. The purpose is to gain insight into what factors led to the employee making that decision and to identify trends or patterns that may indicate changes that need to be made in the workplace. When an employee is terminated due to poor performance or layoff, the employee is likely to have hard feelings towards the company and may have a few choice words to share that will make him/her feel better but won't provide constructive feedback.

Exit interviews may be conducted in a face-to-face conversation or by telephone with an objective representative for the company, preferably a Human Resources professional. Some managers may wish to conduct exit interviews with their departing staff, but employees are not likely to be very forthcoming.

Other options include providing a written survey for the employee to complete or using a computer-based survey. Companies may want to consider allowing employees to submit their responses anonymously if they choose to do so, but this may make it more difficult to determine specific issues that may need to be addressed.

Ideally, Human Resources professionals who are trained in confidentiality and who are experienced in listening to employees' concerns without getting emotional or jumping to conclusions should conduct exit interviews. If this is not an option for your organization because you don't have an internal HR professional on staff, you may want to consider contracting with a Human Resources consultant to provide this service for you.

Section IV
"Must Haves" to Remember...

- Communication is key to avoiding surprises during a termination.

- Lack of documentation is the biggest pitfall during a termination. Lack of documentation can mean the difference between winning and losing an employment case.

- Use exit interviews from employees that exit voluntarily to obtain valuable information to improve your organization.

V. Other Must-Haves

Job Descriptions

Organizations must have some basic documents to work properly. Job descriptions are one of those "must-haves". Job descriptions set the foundation by determining based on the employees responsibilities whether they are exempt or non-exempt, simultaneously determining whether an employee is eligible or ineligible for overtime.

In addition, job descriptions are a good way to convey expectations. It is important to determine a mutual understanding of the job between the employee and their direct report. Without a clear road map, it will be difficult to determine what deliverables to expect from an employee. Job descriptions should not be too descriptive in a way that limits the imagination of the employee nor condensed in a way that makes it vague.

Job descriptions are crucial for employers for various reasons. Of these reasons, is finding the right candidates, minimizing overlaps between different jobs, and having the ability to weigh each job. Once an employer can efficiently determine the weight of the job this can contribute to cutting pay inflation, increasing employee retention, and establishing an effective organizational structure.

New Hire Orientations

One of the most critical aspects of any new hire orientation is the reading and signing of the company's employee handbook. This Human Resources bible outlines all pertinent policies relating to the employee's new place of employment.

The reading of the employee handbook is but the first step. Whether it is three days or 30 days, the planning of a proper orientation procedure for new employees is critical to reducing performance problems and employee turnover.

It all starts with engagement. It's not just a matter of making sure the employee's workspace is ready, badges prepared, and email and other administrative considerations handled. Another critical component of the new hire orientation process is determining the type of work the employee will be assigned. This sort of pro-active work assignment should be part of a larger effort to nurture new employees. The costs of employee turnover range from 30% to 100% of a new hire's first year's pay. So it benefits both the company and the employee to make a new worker feel as if they are part of the team from the first day.

Section V
"Must Haves" to Remember...

• Job descriptions provide a road map for employees. It is the foundation to a strong and effective organizational structure.

• New hire orientations should include the review and signing of your company's Employee Handbook. A proper new orientation is critical to reducing performance problems and employee turnover.

VI.   You Need an HR Partner

In closing, managing humans can be an extremely daunting task.   If you are a small business with 10,000 employees or less, it is beneficial to have an on-site HR person on your staff to handle day-to-day questions and issues as they arise.   Unfortunately, employees in administrative roles are usually not equipped to answer complicated human resources questions or make decisions based on knowledge of federal and state employment laws.   I began my career in an administrative role and how much I did not know as I was providing advice and counsel to employees during that time should have frightened the entire organization!   If you cannot afford to hire a full time HR person and/or HR staff, hire a consultant.

VII.   References & Acknowledgements

1.   The SHRM Learning System, 2005 Version, Module 5, Employee and Labor Relations.

2.   HR for Small Business- From hiring to firing and everything in between,1st edition, 2005, Charles H. Fleisher, Attorney At Law, Sphinx Publishing.

3.   Verdicts & Settlements, December 21, 2009: Hollister Co. wins suit over dress code, Donna Walter, Publication: Missouri Lawyers Media

4.   http://www.EEOC.gov

5.   http://www.whitehouse.gov/healthreform

6.   http://www.IRS.Gov

7.   http://SHRM.org

8.   http://www.nlrb.gov

9.   http://www.USAToday.com

10.   http://www.osha.gov

About the Author

Thelá R. Thatch, MBA, PHR has over 20 years of business and HR experience. Her experience began at Fox TV in NY where she was instrumental in interviewing and training production interns and assistants. She has worked for Bill Cosby Productions, NBC, Cablevision, Paychex, ADC, Devro and UPS. As an HR Consultant, she audits business practices, procedures and creates Employee Handbooks while advising and coaching numerous small, medium and non-profit businesses in all areas of HR. Thatch was an Adjunct Professor within Strayer's School of Business where she taught HR courses. She is well-known for her passion for diversity, employee relations skills, mediation techniques, and her writing and speaking ability. A freelance writer and blogger, she volunteers with several non-profit organizations and serves on the board of the National Association of African Americans in HR. If you are interested in having **Thelá** address your organization visit **www.MRSHR.com** or send an email to **tthatch@mrshr.com**.